poems

THE OPPOSITE HOUSE

CLAUDIA EMERSON

Louisiana State University Press   Baton Rouge

Published by Louisiana State University Press
Copyright © 2015 by Claudia Emerson
All rights reserved
Manufactured in the United States of America
First printing

Designer: Barbara Neely Bourgoyne
Typeface: Whitman
Printer and binder: Thomson-Shore, Inc.

Library of Congress Cataloging-in-Publication Data

Emerson, Claudia, 1957–
  [Poems. Selections]
  The opposite house : poems / Claudia Emerson.
      pages ; cm. — (Southern messenger poets)
  ISBN 978-0-8071-5847-0 (cloth : alk. paper) — ISBN 978-0-8071-5848-7 (pbk. : alk. paper) —
  ISBN 978-0-8071-5849-4 (pdf) — ISBN 978-0-8071-5850-0 (epub) — ISBN 978-0-8071-5851-7 (mobi)
  I. Title.
  PS3551.N4155A6 2015
  811'.54—dc23

                                                            2014022575

For Bunny

There's been a Death, in the Opposite House,
As lately as Today—
I know it, by the numb look
Such Houses have—alway—

—EMILY DICKINSON

CONTENTS

ONE

Ephemeris

The household sells in a morning, but when
they cannot let the house itself go for
the near-nothing it brings at auction,
the children, all beyond their middle years,
carry her back to it, the mortgage now
a dead pledge of patience. Almost emptied,
there is little evidence that she ever
lived in it: a rented hospital bed
in the kitchen where the breakfast table
stood, a borrowed coffee pot, chair,
a cot for the daughter she knows, and then does not.
But the world seems almost right, the near-
familiar curtainless windows, the room
neat, shadow-severed, her body's thinness,
like her gown's, a comfort now. Perhaps
she thinks it death and the place a lesser
heaven, the hereafter a bed, the night
to herself, rain percussive in the gutters—
enough. But like hers, the light sleep of spring
has worsened—forsythia blooming
in what should be deep winter outside
the window—until it resembles the shallow
sleep of a house with a newborn in it,
a middle child she never saw, a boy
who lived not one whole day (an afternoon?
an evening?) sixty years ago in late
August. And as though born without a mouth,
like a summer moth, he never suckled
and was buried without a name. She had waked to that—
that cusp of summer, crape myrtles' clotted
blooms languishing, anemic, the cicadas
exuberant as they have always been
in their clumsy dying.
                              This middle-born
is now the nearer, no, the only child.
The undertaker's wife has not bathed

and dressed him; the first day's night instead
has passed, quickening into another
day, and another, and he is again awake,
his fist gripping a spindle of turned light,
and he is ravenous in his cradle of air.

Greengrocer

Having made the maze of cartons, bins,
and scales, he moves aproned, unseen among them,
the architectures his to build and rebuild,
pyramids of waxy fruit stickered,
tattooed—out of season and in, exotic
and ordinary. He bends over peaches
and berries, culling out by sight the overripe
netted pears, the lettuces. The color
of clotted cream in this low light, braids
of garlic, snake-fat, suspend from the ceiling,
herbs misted beneath them, spray finer than fog.
Customers handle all of what he has displayed,
worried, he has come to think, skeptical,
the way they might be about a child
they have conceived or might adopt, as though
anxious for a scan, some document
to guarantee what they will find when they cut
into what cannot be returned.
                                        If ever
asked, he would suggest watermelon,
nestled in a bed of clearest ice, halved
and quartered, weighed, and wrapped in a thin membrane
of plastic—briefest preserve of the cleaved seedlessness
for which he knows they will pay more.

House Sparrows

They are here, in the eaves, the clothesline pole,
hayloft—everywhere she looks—and everywhere
she goes they are there before her, in town,
in streetlamps, hooded stoplights, in letters
at the pharmacy, cursive, neon serifs.
She knows they prefer human-made hollows,
though she finds them also in the branches
of evergreens and hawthorns. She entices
the nieces and nephews, whom she dislikes
in equal measure, with a Sunday afternoon's
escape from themselves, and so they learn
to follow her while she spots a nest, then
knocks it down with the longest pole on the place.
They race to the small-domed thing to break it
open like a present, unwrap outer
layers of twigs and roots, tear past the middle
membrane of woven grass, sometimes scraps
of cloth, to find the warm, innermost lining
of feathers. If there is a clutch of eggs
speckled bluish-white, they have learned
to throw them against the barn's wall,
where they explode into a constellation
of watery stars.
                    If there are hatchlings,
the children, delighted, toss them, one after
the other, into the chicken yard—where
she has despised most of all the bold greed
with which the birds steal feed. The chickens,
who have never minded sparrows, fight
each other for every tender-boned, sweet
scream of rarest meat fallen into the lot
they will return to keeping grassless
as a cemetery swept clean of grief.

Clearcut

A Wounded Deer—leaps highest—
—EMILY DICKINSON

Her body is already harvested
of its children, its quickness, both breasts, its work,
most worry, all regret, the intervale
of sorrow behind her now. They planted
the loblollies for this, the old age they had
faith in, hers alone. Neighbors despair
that she would make wasted acres where
those trees had stood for so long they believed them
ownerless given. But if let be, they would
sicken and fail, he had said, all at one,
slowed once.
                    And so the men begin cutting,
inescapable the sound of chainsaw
cough and stutter, the felling, men calling out
to one another as though desperate
for something, the drag of chained logs through mud,
engines downshifting for days, weeks,
the stench of resin, gas, sawdust, oil,
exhaust. Then, the controlled burn, smoke fog-close
to the ground, wafting toward and then away from
the house, before the quiet of replanting
seedlings, trees she does not bother to
imagine.
                    Deer return to the yard, preferring
apples still hanging over those easier
fallen in the shadowy grasses; she watches
a doe's slow rise on hind legs as though in a freezing
leap, not of the wounded but of the resolved,
in its mouth what looks like a small sphere
of sweetest ice. Beyond it, she is able
to take in the main road, a broader swath
of sky, a mile of air—that much clarity.

Lightning

He hears the strike that splits the pecan tree,
sensing the sudden expanse of sky
only as light object-like
in the house. And he hears—the tearing
of grass a sound so much itself—
the cow in the yard before
he sees it, a gate open across
the field, he figures, or a fence
down.
    Its body mere shape, its color
he recalls as weathered marble,
cratered light, the fluid muscle
that makes no allusion to bone.
When the creature lowers its head
to graze in what had been the sky's
highest branches, it becomes them—
both form and insatiable void.

Scarecrow at the Forks of Buffalo

Late afternoon and the house is shut up
tight against night, the thready stream of smoke
that of a lesser fire, early-banked.
The husband, then, must be dead, or so long
gone she does not despair, the scarecrow
wearing his hunting jacket and watch cap,
red-blaze the only color that will burn
through the hour. Beneath the jacket, the figure
wears one of her nightgowns, sleep-thinned—or
sheer from sleeplessness, and still she could not
bear to throw it out farther than this
rough form from which she hung pie pans
one morning, shying in the breeze. Like scales
of some failed justice, they balance now
above the frozen plot, above the crows
that have lost all caution, the sound their wings
make near-vowel as they fly low to land
in ice-choked rows, to peck at hoarfrost,
frozen mud.
              She is in bed but wakeful,
listening, not to crows, but to the faint fork
of the creek winter narrowed but quickened,
and the fainter but fevered keening of dogs
somewhere, scent-pitched, bodiless as though distance
itself had a voice and desire—the garden a seed
catalog, open on the kitchen table, that
one light she left on downstairs fixed on it.

Torch

The tumor was pressed deep into the brain's
left hemisphere, unreachable, like most
of what she thought she had forgotten or stored
reasonably away—the children's things,
the years of the war, her youth, what she felt
about any of it. Her husband, a physician
who had been first a pilot, did not try
to make her think this was a thing that could
be fixed. This the man whose narratives she could
recount word for word, his survival of numberless
night raids that put all of London in the cellar,
how he belly-landed three bombers,
the ways he outlived nine entire flight crews.
Her short-term memory dissolved first,
and she could not recall whether or not
she had eaten, or what he said yesterday,
or that morning. She had to hear the diagnosis
over and over. Her granddaughter disappeared
into someone she had never seen before.
She did not know her daughter. Speech
faded away; the English she learned late
left first. The englassed rooms and the mountains'
changing sameness outside them refused complete
silence for a few more weeks, and even
when those first, lingering words dissolved, she nodded,
sometimes, as though she understood:
                                        She is

in an underground train station, the war on,
the city above the tunnel another blackout.
She has put her flashlight in her raincoat
pocket that blunts the beam she has, without
knowing, left on. What would have been the small
forgettable mistake, he will notice, striding
somehow without sound toward her, to pause,
wordless. When the man who will be the father
of her unimagined children does speak,
it will be to whisper in the delicate shadow
of her ear—to switch it off—and so she will.

Charting the Particulars

He reads it every morning. Like a mapmaker,
he must plot extremes before he can focus
on details, and the extreme of every day
is that the leg is gone, stubborn surprise
because the brain has never accepted it
and still sends down the most ludicrous
of commands, an itch on the missing shin, tickle
on the arch of a foot gone fifty years. Details
come down to rash, pinch, bruise, any flaw that might
prevent him from wearing the thing that leans
in the corner by the bed, ready before him,
in yesterday's sock and shoe, knee locked, bucket
yawning like the mouth of a catfish, landed
and gaping. Some days, in charting the particulars,
it reminds him of one of his children newborn,
before he had reason to dislike it.
                                    He knew,
of course, that it was his, but found it alien
anyway—small, pale, hairless as this
small thing made hairless and pale. And he held it
the way he holds this now, at arm's length, gently
in his two hands, finding nothing familiar
at all, touching it, tenderly, this same way.

Love Bird

By what migration it appeared
in her garden—escape, release—
she will never know and has learned
not to question. Now, beneath
the skylight's slim display of distance,
it flies from the loom in her living
room to the glass rim of the jar
she fills in winter with nandina,
then back again.
                    She would spoil it
with crumbs from her biscuit
but it prefers the teacup's steep
lip, its hunger for the small
rubies embedded in the ring
she still wears, the irresistible—if
impossible—bright, inedible seed.

Darling

She misses the classes but occupies everyone's
office hours; knees hugged up tight against
her chest, she rocks lightly in a straight-back chair,
then lingers in the doorway past whatever
question she makes believe she had, her laughter
decorative, another piercing. She wears
her grandmother's watch on a chain, its only
measure her breathing as she recites her many

sonnets. Gaunt, she swaddles herself in gauzy
scarves, jeans sewn tight against her calves in bright,
neat stitches; she reports cutting herself
out of them at night, another rule she follows
strictly, wildly, as though to perfect, or punish
the darling form she has mistaken for self.

Linguist

She is dying for so long she can, even now,
forget it is so, though her bed is in the dining room,
and she cannot climb the stairs.
                                    Her mother, a lace-
maker in Greece, earned more money than her father
ever did, so insisted she learn piecework, too,
disallowing her the idle hands and idle
tongue of the sea in the mornings, mornings that became
all thread and text, tapestries that forced her
to be still behind a needle-loom,
a vertical screen that closed her in a little more
with the dense stitch of each day.
                                    So, she sewed
an ocean, and an island's edge, sea-carved
cliff, no narrative in them beyond
a child's thread of longing.
                                    They are sheer narrative
now, framed and hung here, her mother's airy lace—
its beauty patterned absence—kept inside
the glass cabinets surrounding her.
                                    The real sea
is kept as it always was for afternoon,
and afternoon's edge is its own language,
waves the weft-faced push and pull, syllable
and salt-laced syntax the tide she plunges,
herself the needle, now, the needle's lyric eye.

Third

He survived the first beach landing and an entire
world war for this: the textile mill, buildings
looming over the river, windows painted
black during the war so they could run the third
shift he came to choose—easier he found
to black out the days, shutter them, so that the hours
that had been for drinking or the dreams
he could better sleep through, to wake evenings
for cigarettes and coffee. The trick—not to wake
too much, avoid the gaze of the face in the mirror
as he shaved it, watch static on the television screen
or the crosshairs of a test pattern. Nights were
easier bright and loud—rooms the size
of airplane hangars, close as circus tents,
dye room, spinning room, his the weave room,
voiceless, lit with sound, rows of looms,
their ceaseless weft and warp, shuttles swift,
percussive—clawhammer-like—air thick
with the smell of cotton, lint in their lungs, their hair,
sheeting like dyed, transfigured fields, or fields
bleached to blinding, a collective shroud.
                                          Graveyard shift
made them all equal, orphaned; those with families
saw them Sundays, afternoon its own ghost.
It was easier to bear what no one else wanted—
a world just lightening when his shift ended, the river
they all crossed running with the night's dye.

Induction

The porch light burns all one morning,
all that afternoon and the next,
unnoticed, like a day moon. The cat
appears—a skittish persistence
at a neighbor's door. A nightgown hangs
on the line, heavy with rain, then
stiffens in the wind. Azaleas bloom
livid, hot inside the bedsheets
she used to swaddle them against
a late frost everyone else
has forgotten. Mail clots the box.

Entrance

1.

Some evenings her own house convinces her
she is already dead, photographs framed
portals into which she sometimes falls
awake in another room. The phone is silent
in its cradle, food tasteless, even salt dumb
grains of glass. She calls someone who does answer
but a voice cannot convince her otherwise,
the self dead who called another woman's
husband with an innocent question the excuse
to hear his voice, the self who would have had
a cigarette about now, the lighter in a drawer
here somewhere, her initials engraved, a flourish
of cursive. She craved the sound of the thumbwheel's
scrape against flint, small flame, that first long drag,
the practiced rings of smoke she formed with a mouth
painted to disappear behind them. The glass
of driest sherry cannot persuade her, though
she drinks it anyway. Her hair, her fingernails,
her nakedness against the naked floor, the body
unbathed for days, some days, not enough.

2.

Too small to see into the upper nests,
she feels the sleeve of its body well muscled
with eggs. She knows her mother's fury
will be not only at the eggs lost,
but at the setting egg devoured also,
a doorknob of oblong, crazed porcelain
meant to trick the hens into laying.
She would have tried to kill the snake anyway,
but now has to be more certain of it,
lifting out the stuporous body
and quickly, deftly, severing the head,
offensive mouth with a paring knife

the way she has been taught. She massages out
a fluid wasteful braid of whites and yolks
shell-specked—what would have been more than enough,
she thinks, for a pound cake—before the knob
at last falls with a thud, like anything
but an egg, to the ground: small insistent
entrance to another house, any house,
a painted door, and, all to herself, one fool room.

TWO

EARLY ELEGIES

Headmistress

The word itself: prim, retired, its artifact
her portrait above the fireplace, on her face
the boredom she abhorred, then perfected,
her hands held upward—their emptiness
a revision, cigarette and brandy snifter
painted, intolerably, out, to leave her this
lesser gesture: *What next?* or shrugged *Whatever*.
From the waist down she was never there.

Telephone Booth

Its remains: a plexiglass crypt robbed
of confession, apology, despair, its half
of all conversation now a narrow
column of strictest clarity, a coinless
reliquary where the receiver dangles
like an unwatched hook, and the phonebook
hangs from its chain—obedient
to the numbered gravity of names.

Cursive

Children train instead the small muscles
in their hands to strike—uniform, precise—
preformed fonts of their choice. Frail evidence
of ornamental scripts (and cloven nibs, hairline
serifs), the signature, still required, survives,
though poorly executed, its likely demise
the scan of a single fingertip—loops, inkless
whorls—one, incorruptible exemplar.

Barber

Scissors and straight razors he keeps honed
in case—sits in one of the chairs facing
a wall of empty mirrors reflecting mirrors
behind him, the backs of his head, one after
the shrunken, redundant other. Finally,
with a towel, he covers the television screen
mounted on the wall, the way he might—nearing
the end of day—a parakeet in a cage.

Operator

Or perhaps this is for the stubbornly imagined,
supposed self, simply on break, on the bench
outside, unwrapping wax paper from a sandwich.
All morning she has answered, ever pleasant,
the one no one wants, but must reach for the sheer
conduit she is. And she already knows
she has become this: zero, dial-less cipher, this
free half-hour from which she will not return.

Drive-In Movie Theater

One of the last was *The South*. The owner
resorted finally to x-rated films
and an all-girl staff at the concession stand
where a man would wait in line for a sweaty
bottle of beer and a pricey bucket of wings,
his car parked beneath the screen filled
with the sky-high obvious he would pretend,
in that obscene exchange, he did not see.

Wisdom Teeth

They arrive, if at all, late, awkward, huddled
in the back, crowding the hinges of the jaw—
pain their remaining purpose, the revenge
of the body's forgetfulness. The eviction
lifts them from dull slumber into the sterile,
expensive chamber of the needle and knife
where they hit stainless steel with the ring of bullets dug,
one after the other, from the same old wound.

Smallpox

The world has certified itself rid of
all but the argument: to eradicate or not
the small stock of *variola* frozen,
quarantined—a dormancy it has
refused, just once, for a woman behind a sterile
lens, her glass slide a clearest, most
becoming pane. How could it resist slipping
away with her, that discrete first pock?

THREE

Lock

After the Emily Dickinson traveling exhibit at the Folger Shakespeare Library,
Washington, D.C., 12 April 2012

I noticed the quick wore off those things . . .
—EMILY DICKINSON, ON DAGUERREOTYPES

The evening includes a reception, wine
and hors d'oeuvres with the curator, lighthearted
discussion of the various diagnoses,
hypotheses long debated—depression,
lesbianism, grief, agoraphobia,
the kind of anxiety a cat has
about the threshold, and the most recent
theory—epilepsy; that would explain it
all, they say, spasmodic punctuation,
reclusiveness, the shame, everything,
the hour of lead, at last, unlocked.
                                    On display:
one of her beloved nephew Gilbert's
boyhood suits, velveteen, and beside it
the contents of his morning's pocket—a bullet's
spent casing, a wad of tangled string; drafts
of more famous poems bearing clearly
the needle-piercings where she sewed one
to another—the sutures of a fascicle's
finishing undone; what is thought to be
the only image ever made of her,
of which she disapproved, here, itself,
as yet without compare;
                            and next to it,
the something rare, unexpected, lock
of her hair—the shape and circumference
reminiscent of a sparrow's nest, the color
she likened to a chestnut bur. She had brushed,
cut, coiled, and folded it into an envelope,
then sent it to someone, letter-like. Everyone
lines up to photograph it with their phones,

when what they must truly desire is to
touch it, as though they might feel the sheen
it retains. And while they can never
get close enough, they will never be any
closer than this to what it does not tell them,
and they are desperate for all that that might mean.

The Opposite House

This place:
        a cavernous warehouse
                of houses
dismantled,
        cataloged,
            reordered here
according
        to part-rendered-
            particle—
elemental—
        the sentient
           stuff of space
stored in meta-
        space: this
           room for doors,
thresholds,
        staircases, risers
           and stretchers,
banisters hand-
        worn-smooth; this
           for scrollwork,
moldings—egg
        and tongue; for
           floorboards—tongue
in groove; this
        room for windows,
           sills, sashes,
transoms; this
        for mantles, shadow-
           scents
of dead fires;
        this a room
           of bins: hinges,
doorknobs,
        latches, locks. All
           of it aged,

orphaned—
                artifacts of the
                            slower fires
of neglect,
            abandonment, before
                            bone-
pickers raced
            the demolition for what
                            might be
salvaged to sell
            again, like
                    prizing gold
from the teeth
            of the dead, to be
                            re-measured, leveled,
grafted as though
            re-made into
                    the agelessness
of someone else's
            household-now.
                            As long
as they are
            here, though, the fact
                    of every door
remains
        reference to
                    an antecedent made
vague—a
        cellar hole an
                    empty socket
somewhere, or
            a sandy lot
                    opposite some
newer house,
        a sidewalk's
                    stones' arrival

into grass,
          or daffodils blooming
                    like wild,
unmeant things
          in what
                appears an old field
without design,
          the kind
              sumac prefers
and will
        encircle—its
             own transfiguring
salvage,
       that—slow,
          unambiguous.

Rural Letter Carrier

For a brief while, the eighty-six miles gave some
illusion of travel, the seasons' slow
cycling part of it—the sky moving
from cloud to clearing, fields turned under
or crowded with corn, crows, soybeans, tobacco,
snow. But the road did not change, finally—
not the straight stretches, nor rain-fretted curves,
the relentless echo of gravel-ping, the hushing
of dust, mud-hiss and skunk-musk. The houses
went down over time, the men dying away,
then the widows; in the yards of emptied houses,
their children went on living in trailers with tires
on the roofs. And the names on the mailboxes
and the ones in the ragged graveyards were
the same. Some people hung their clothes from barbwire
fences to dry, and as long as I had been driving
that route delivering her check, one old woman
still hid behind the trunk of a sycamore
in her yard until I drove off again. Some days,
I stopped at the country store where a few bottles
of soda floated like blasted fish in the drinkbox,
where men checked deer and turkeys and bought bait,
where no one knew any news but of who died.
It only took my Sunday absence for a wren
or sparrow to begin a nest in a mailbox
forgotten open, or a hornet to finish one
that I'd find hanging down like a gray wattle
or venomous goiter from the throat.
They said there wouldn't be letters anymore,
what with people getting news through the air,
and money just numbers on a screen
that added up to a worse nothing, stored
in a machine somewhere—all of it invisible
and flying reckless, swarmless as thoughts
never meant to be spoken, then spoken.

I had driven through enough lonely
days to believe sometimes I passed by those hours
instead, like estranged houses to which I might
return some distant day, not to deliver
a day's worries and ordinary temptations—
but the letter addressed in a hand so far away,
so familiar, it would need no other understanding,
having found in me its last and only way.

Common House Sparrows at JFK's International Terminal

They survive in factories, warehouses,
even coalmines; some were, after all, ship-borne,
and so that they are here should not surprise,
their small host a constant nervousness—
accepted, ignored—around and about
the food court's balcony, just above
security. From their perch—a skeletal
sculpture of abstracted aluminum
and guy-wire—they seek breadcrumbs, grains of rice,
of salt and sugar strewn beneath tables
and chairs, their survival dependent
on redundant carelessness.
                          Perhaps they are not
captive here and meant to enter—through
an air vent or skylight; or, perhaps,
they succumbed to curiosity
and the happenstance of the automatic doors'
slow revolve to become the only natives
of this place, everyone else transient,
destinations ticketed, mirage-like.
They bask in what light manages to fall
through soot-fogged windows, or bathe in the slough
of neverending passage, arrivals
and departures in perfected synchrony—this
windless, rainless asylum sky enough.

Practice Blood

From late spring through summer, the county paper
runs grainy photographs of anomalies
from gardens, an entire page—tomatoes big
as melons held up by people who grew them,
conjoined pumpkins, the absurd, misshapen gourd.
But when hunting season opens, a full page
won't hold them: first turkey, first doe, first buck,
killed by boys mostly, though not all, children
as young as six or seven holding gobblers
by the feet, wing spans wider than they are
tall, others posed holding up bucks' heads
by their antlers. The day comes long awaited,
inevitable as the wedding on another page.
They cannot recall when the first of the opened
carcasses appeared suspended from the tree
beside the swing. They were told the joy of it
before being waked up to see the gutting,
dressing, before being brought along to watch,
all part of practicing: *inhale, exhale*
by half, squeeze, don't pull. The captions name
whose child, whose land, what make, caliber—shotgun,
muzzleloader, rifle, sometimes detail
about the kill, the points in the rack's expanse,
a dropped tine.
    All their eyes are open,
as though in compliance, wet, luminous—the same
whether heart shot and dropped mid-graze or lung shot,
found hours later having tried to outrun the blood-
raveling wound; the lens of the eye still shines
as though from dawn fog, or the field of frost
after the understory died—exhaled by half—
this the look of a mirror in a vacant house
that seems to hold a light no longer there.

Dr. Crawford Long, Discoverer of the First Surgical Anesthetic, and the Case of Isam Bailey

Jefferson County, Georgia, 8 January 1845

I had already performed the experiment,
removed a tumor from the neck of a friend,
James Venable; when he woke he thought I
had not yet begun. I had to show it
to him, big as a quail's egg, let him
touch the fresh, wet stitches.
       The hand of God
came later when a neighborwoman brought me
a boy called Isam, one of her slaves, two fingers
ruined from a burn she had neglected. Needless
loss; had she brought him to me sooner I might have
been able to save them, but mortification
had set in, and she was worried now
about the loss of the arm, more than half
the value of a boy in the bargain.
        The only
implement needed was the metacarpal
blade; I recall its mirror-finish particularly
bright in January light. I recall the quiet,
almost unnerving. This was the simplest
of amputations, though, taking off a finger
just above the knuckle, and I worked
at the same speed I would have had he been
awake—no need to linger in it. When I
roused him to the news that it was already gone,
he didn't believe me—and I had to show him
the hand, the finger itself, and still he did not
quite believe. But perhaps I had Mesmerized him,
skeptics would say, the mere suggestion
of ether-laced cloth placed like a shroud
over his nose and mouth enough to cast
a simple black child into a stupor.

And so, to demonstrate that he was not
merely suggestible to me, I removed
the other finger without it. He felt it,
of course, as I knew he would—and I found
myself working even more quickly to hasten it,
though I was accustomed to such displays
of pain—and knew his would be brief, that small
bone insensible, easy to prune
as wisteria at the root.
                              His owner signed
a certificate of witness, and Isam
would talk about it for the rest of his life,
those small, neatened nubs stories he would
always tell apart, the fingers consumed
not by one but two fires—one he could feel
and hear, the searing cut, pull, quick-snapping
pass of the blade, the other deathless,
dreamless oblivion, sleep that refused
measure.
            I suppose it might be compared
to the womb—known place and time no one can recall
and so can never forget, where fingers
are knit, webbed to the hand, Isam's for this;
and this was no experiment, but a miracle by design,
a proof—like a Lazarus—and I had performed it.

Virginia Christian

The first female electrocuted in the state of Virginia in 1912, Virginia Christian was a
17-year-old African American maid who killed her white employer, the widow Ida Belote,
after an argument that ensued when Belote accused Christian of stealing a locket. Belote's
cruelty was well documented, and though Christian was a minor, the prosecution argued
that her physical maturity have bearing on her sentencing.

A lynching gathering,
        a horizon closing in,
                the men
would hurry
      to do it, send her
          to a black man's
death, arguing
      that the widow
          had been *frail, delicate,*
while Virginia
      they called *full-blooded—*
           a *negress* with eyes
dark, lusterless.
     They reported her
          to have a black man's
appetite, a black
     man's sleep,
        untroubled, sound
as though from some
      hard labor. She
          waited for it five months,
listening to lawyers
     talk about writs
       and appeals
in a cell from which
     she was able—
       unable not—to see
clearly into the small
     chamber, the scaffold
        of the electric

chair, newly made

from a single tree,

the stiff leather

harnesses she would

wear. There was only

her account of it,

that they had each

taken up one

of the severed broom

handles that held

open the bedroom

windows—(salvage

of how many floors

swept, hallways,

corners), which must have

fallen to shut in

the argument, sharp

blades, one after

the other. It ended

when Virginia

shoved a towel

and with it

the woman's tongue and

some of her hair

down her throat

with a poker, she

said, to stop it.

Then she did take

a ring, a purse—some

coins, and in

the stunned

reprieve of a spring

afternoon was seen

buying penny candy,

the woman not

dead, she swore,

but quiet she had
       left her as
           the slow, inevitable
dissolve of those
       last few hours.
           The one photograph
of her—taken
       at the penitentiary after
           the sentence—
composes upper
       body, her face, the set
           of the mouth,
the inexpressible
       quick in her
           eyes, part unbelief,
part the look
       of distance, as though
           the camera's
flash crazed
       the black glaze
           of a sky that was to come
as it always did
       with August, the strike
           they would harness
for her, send
       into her brain a thing
           she could not have
imagined, one cloven
       tongue enough
           to light forever
the house she would never
       again see, enough
           to light the city.
She was not born
       dead, but buried—
           in the slow certain

strike of
        conception, the quickening
                into another
girlchild too black—
           in a white woman's
                  house, her widowed
wrath and washing,
          in the locket (chain
                and hinge, chambered
image, perhaps
        a strand of hair) she
              did or did not
steal—buried
        in a body having early
            turned on her,
in the fullness of her own
          breasts, belly,
             and thighs—her grave
the bed where
        she was born, the very
            air, her first
drawn breath
        the casting down
           of a fistful of earth.

Apologue

Don't imagine this as anything
beyond the old arc snapped, covenant entirely
broken, our ships no more than silver needles
trying the boundless haystacks of the stars.
—FROM "FALLEN," BY BETTY ADCOCK

Long before the shining capsule, swaying
like a seed, splashed into the ocean, and they
reappeared from it bearded and waving, the men
sent animals—the way they had birds
and mules into mineshafts—first into orbit
and then deep space beyond it: anaesthetized,
harnessed, electrodes in their brains—another
kind of husbandry. Chimpanzees, cats,
tortoises, dogs, rats, rabbits, pigs, silkworms,
salamanders, bees—spiders to see
if they would weave, eggs to see if they would hatch.
All of it in search of what might be
workable for themselves in artificial air,
weatherless time, in a gravity-suspended
replica of light. They watched from behind
the blinds of telescopes, lenses, clipboards,
slide rules—theirs the atmosphere of a nervous
curiosity.
      The void beyond them
they claimed—the way they always had—as some
better, necessary place in the face
of ruin, of greed, the cosmos a floodlessness,
the wilderness a cleaner thicket of stars,
something they thought they knew by naming,
by seeing themselves, their fables dying
in the patterns. Desperate to reach it, after
the animals burned, they, too, burned at the launches,
or exploded to atomize like a virga
that hangs, drifts, and never reaches the earth.

When the space shuttle disintegrated over
East Texas, the bodies of astronauts were scattered
piecemeal all over the Big Thicket; searchers
tried to salvage the dismembered strewn
amongst the wreckage and reassemble them
in the sanctuary of a church—first, to save them
from being devoured by wild boars, then
in an attempt to knit them again to a name,
by fingerprint, DNA from a lock
of hair—nothing left but samples.

                            Something
did survive the fire, though, the fall, some
small canistered experiment involving
free-living creatures thin as eyelashes
recovered alongside a severed hand
still gloved, head helmeted; a form the size
of a comma was let fall to that violent
reversal of the garden, unharmed, fated
to return to the laboratory's tests and trials:
C. elegans, common nematode, wild ecology
unknown, named from the Greek for *thread*,
spin, *needle*, and *form*—bewildering,
what notion they will take from it.

Limb Factory

—The hand of the LORD was upon me, and carried me out in the
spirit of the LORD, and set me down in the midst of the valley which
was full of bones, And caused me to pass by them round about: and,
behold, there were very many in the open valley; and, lo, they were
very dry. And he said unto me, Son of man, can these bones live?
And I answered, O Lord GOD, thou knowest.
　　　—EZEKIEL 37: 1–3

Despite
　　　the seeming
　　　　　　singularity of the fetal
sonogram—
　　　　the wonder, or
　　　　　　　despair,
at a murky,
　　　　undeniable first,
　　　　　　　an avoided,
or longed-for,
　　　　windfall last—
　　　　　　　perhaps all
of it has been
　　　like this
　　　　　mass production,
an assembly
　　　line, the demand
　　　　　　a given,
though more,
　　　　in this place,
　　　　　　　in times of war:
the industry of it
　　　　a study
　　　　　　in loss,
and the argument
　　　　against it,
　　　　　　　the physics

48

and engineering

       of what

           moves, recovers,

resists, and follows

       the body's

          original order,

the flux and give

       of a gathering

          of dust

reproduced piecemeal—

       a room for arms,

            legs, someone's

specialty

    the knee,

       the foot, someone's

the hand. And

      perhaps such

         survival has always been

part conjure,

      part clinical,

        the muscle twitch

of quickening

     a fashioned thing,

         interchangeable—

abject this remembrance,

       not begotten—

          made.

Irene Virga Salafia

Alfredo Salafia (1869–1933) was a famous Sicilian embalmer, most well known for
the modern "mummy" Rosalia Lombardo (1918–1920), one of the eight thousand
mummies kept in the Catacombe dei Cappuccini in Palermo, Sicily.

I was his second wife; I understood this,
too, as passion, his days spent with the dead,
months in the making of whatever it was
and would be called, the smell on him at night
not death, the alchemy of God. When he
touched me, I knew I was the stranger flesh—
here-alive, yes, and half his age, young as
his own daughters, younger. And I understood,
too, what preoccupied him so—the unseen
he saw in all things, proofs, solutions, the *whys*
of guttering candles, of wax, of prayer, of the blood
orange he would peel while reading the paper,
the segment he would offer to me, mindless,
juice on his fingers, while, below us, people
coursed the narrow streets to pool in the piazzas,
stones ice-slick beneath them. He understood those
who would not be satisfied with such stone,
a name carved, a face set in bronze, marble—
or with an image, a lock of hair.

                      He thought it
art—far beyond balm—levitation, almost,
that immaculate a suspense, exact
and abstract, the thing itself made other,
italicized. And why not in this city
of sculptures common as the shutters and balconies—
faces on every building, horses on the rooftop
of the theater, angels in every garden,
in every fountain the water carved by stone.
His studio—a laboratory, and in it,
glass vials, needles, chemicals, the marble
slab where they lay.

               In notebooks he recorded
early attempts, the animals—some birds,

mostly dogs—a mosaic of failed equations,
then the bodies unclaimed from the morgue,
then his own brother, father, until
he proved he could do more than preserve,
transforming those weeks gone, like bringing up
the drowned, not to life, but to the surface
from which they had sunk.
                                    His last was a child,
two years old, lost to pneumonia, named
along with countless other little girls
for Rosalia, a hermit who died alone
in a weeping cave, the saint we all prayed to,
who had once banished a plague, her bones kept
unseen in a silver urn in the cathedral.
                                    The child's
cheeks and lips he made plump with injections
of wax—but the unseen-all of her he worked
hardest to preserve—her heart and lungs,
her brain, a darkened closet of zinc salts,
glycerin, acid, formalin where once
there had been the sea, absorbed, and the mountains
enclosing it. Incorruptible, he declared her—
perfect votive, her ribboned hair a spun-gold
cold flame—and tucked her in, her cradle, lead-
lined, its lid wax-sealed glass, its clawed feet
those of an animal, as though she would be
forever borne on the back of a tamed beast.
Was this not love?
                                    Three months after we married,
I would bury him with his first wife and stand
outside the tomb as though orphaned along
with his daughters. Winter, still, the hour was mild;
the almond trees would flush pink in a week
with blossoms.
                                    His cursive perfect, the formula
and instructions for it he would leave behind him,
on the frontispiece below his name, an etching

of Charon ferrying a sleeping woman across
the Styx to the underworld.
                            But the child's place is
the forever of an alcove at the end
of the long crypt, its ceilings vaulted like a capuchin's
deep hood, its passageways lined with weary
corpses stacked in caskets or hung from bolts
sunk in the walls, arranged as though the old
order of sex and class still matters. Their bodies
were drained, emptied, the cavities refilled
with straw, then dressed for another Monday,
all their heads bowed as though peering over
balconies, those deep sills, at the street below me,
where shopkeepers sweep in the morning, the sound
of broomstraw on stone a kind of breathing,
where a blind dog crosses, eyes the colorlessness
of quartz, and the old pick through the day before
heaped reeking on the corner.
                            She will remain
like the odd-alone, small yellow sorrel—most
common of wildflowers—I pressed in the back
of this book, not the stuff of memory unless
I write the hour we sat on a bench of stone,
parrots making green screaming ribbons of the air
above us; I wanted something to remember it by,
some small memento I recall hesitating
to take from its one afternoon of pollen
and bees—color its one remaining trueness,
shape collapsed, thinned as paper—this preserve
a worse kind of withering, perhaps, and yet
you see how I again have turned to it
for its very failure to compare.

The Ocularist

One of the earliest
              eyes was found
                            with the ancient
corpse of a woman
              in Persia, hers
                            made of gold
to resemble
              a small sun—
                            iris and sclera
chased rays—
              clear testament
                            not to the eye,
but to the light
              that had been
                            made go out.
The later ones
              crafted of glass
                            I studied
and practiced
              for fire-blown
                            beauty, learning
another fragility,
              vulnerability
                            to the body's
heat, the way
              glass shatters
                            inside the fleetest
fever. For
              its give—
                            and forgiveness—
I worked then
              in ivory-wax,
                            and after
perfecting the shape,
              cloned with
                            paint an iris,

small blood
           vessels from
                      filaments of red
silk, then sealed
             the whole
                       beneath an acrylic
veneer—thin,
                 invisible. Mine
                     was always
the smaller
              studio, the work
                  fine, lonely
as a jeweler's,
           my needs
                  the same—a window,
a lamp, lighted
               eye loupe. Half-
                     sculptor, half-
illustrator, I
             thought for
                a long time
I was crafting
             something place-
                    saving at best,
an orbit-
           warmed imposter,
                  elegy,
implied
          narrative of loss—
                 flying glass
or knife,
          a thumb's determined
                    gouge. But I
learned finally
            to manipulate
                 the way light

played the sphere—
                    the pupil
                                        seeming to dilate
from dusk or
                    desire—becoming
                                        architect
not of form
                    but of function,
                                        not of object
but of the seen-
                    self, enticing it not
                                        to look away.
The patient's
                    eye took with it,
                                        after all,
only periphery
                    and the perception
                                        of depth,
asides the truest
                    beholding has
                                        never required.
So I aligned
                    the gaze
                                        for the whole-sighted
world, that
                    it might find
                                        some small figment
of itself
                    contained there, already in
                                        the brain—
I could make it
                    believe—the fact
                                        of what was
not there of no
                    matter at all,
                                        the final

measure of an eye's

       worth, in fact,

             its complete

disappearance—

      and with it,

           mine—into

the opposite

     eye that was

        such belief.

A Frontispiece

The hallways, too, have become narrowed
with first editions, forgotten histories,
novels, rare volumes of verse, some hand-sewn,
stitches machine-fine, spines still tightly bound.
He can recall where he found each title,
what he paid, how much he gained or lost
in the purchase. This late delight, though,
a frontispiece, a page translucent with age,
its ornament meaningless as frostwork
inside a window—wordless entrance where
he finds himself lingering, almost as though
outside the house closing in around him.

Not quite a year, he had been old enough
to stand but not walk, and they found him upright,
gripping the bars of the crib, looking calmly,
they told him, over the railing, not at them,
but at the window opened to a world
he could not yet have perceived as below.
He would never be able to recall
how old he was when they first told him
of the suicide, or even who told him,
his mother or one of the aunts, the most important
and agreed-upon detail to all of them
the fact of his presence in the room
from which his father leapt, falling how many
stories to the street. Perhaps he had been asleep
and seen nothing, they said, and had awakened
to voices wafting in on October light.
Or, perhaps, he thought, the man had leaned
over the crib looking for last reason
before disappearing into the child's
perception: air that did not yet possess
gravity, or language, or despair.

ACKNOWLEDGMENTS

For their encouragement while writing this book, I give great thanks to my husband, Kent Ippolito; my mother, Mollie Emerson; and friends and colleagues Betty Adcock and Rod Smith. I offer special thanks to Catherine MacDonald for being first reader. The Governor's School English classes in Stafford, Virginia, that I visited in January 2012 gave me particularly helpful advice about "A Frontispiece."

And I am particularly grateful to the Guggenheim Foundation for a fellowship in support of this work, to series editor Dave Smith and all of the staff at Louisiana State University Press for their ongoing belief in me—as well as to my colleagues and friends at the Sewanee Writers' Conference for yearly inspiration.

Many thanks to the editors of the following magazines in which these poems appeared, some in slightly different form: *Birmingham Poetry Review*: "Apologue," "Clearcut," "Common House Sparrows at JFK's International Airport," "Lightning," "Third," and "Virginia Christian"; *Blackbird*: "Irene Virga Salafia," "Limb Factory," "The Ocularist," and "The Opposite House"; *Chronicle of Higher Education*: "Ephemeris"; *Cortland Review*: "A Frontispiece," "Charting the Particulars," "Entrance," "Practice Blood," "Rural Letter Carrier," and "Scarecrow at the Forks of Buffalo"; *The New Yorker*: "Early Elegy: Barber"; *Poetry*: "Early Elegy: Headmistress" and "Early Elegy: Smallpox"; *Plume*: "Early Elegy: Cursive," "Early Elegy: Drive-In Movie Theater," "Early Elegy: Operator," "Early Elegy: Telephone Booth," "Early Elegy: Wisdom Teeth"; *Shenandoah*: "Dr. Crawford Long, Discoverer of the First Surgical Anesthetic, and the Case of Isam Bailey," "Linguist," and "Love Bird"; *Southern Poetry Review*: "Darling," "Induction," "Lock," and "Torch"; *Virginia Quarterly Review*: "Greengrocer" and "House Sparrows."

NOTES

"Torch" is for Trudy Fox.

"Linguist" is for Christina Kakava.

"Virginia Christian" owes much of its historical grounding to "'A Gruesome Warning to Black Girls': The August 16, 1912, Execution of Virginia Christian," by Derryn Eroll Moten.

"Irene Virga Salafia" was inspired by Dario Piombino-Mascali's ongoing work with the mummies in Palermo, Sicily, as well as his book *Il Maestro del Sonno Eterno*. A special thanks to Antonella Dellatorre, for translating from the Italian.